Smartfood

Recipes and Tips for Staying Healthy and Living Longer

WHITE STAR PUBLISHERS

Photographs and Recipes
CINZIA TRENCHI

Project Editor
VALERIA MANFERTO DE FABIANIS

Graphic Layout
VALENTINA GIAMMARINARO

INTRODUCTION

The Properties of Basic Foods and How to Use Them

Recipes

Introduction

What is Smart Food? The European Institute of Oncology (IEO) defines "smart foods" as those rich in bioactive compounds that affect the metabolic pathways linked with longevity. In other words, smart foods are all those which help the body stay healthy for longer and counteract the onset of diseases such as diabetes, obesity, cancer and other cardiovascular and degenerative diseases.

For many years now, numerous Western societies - characterised by a common level of well-being and often by overeating - have been facing an increasingly higher incidence of these diseases, which are not only expensive for the individual, but also for the family and the entire community. Not surprisingly, therefore, research has been focused on prevention, seeking to identify the most correct eating habits to prevent such diseases.

Over the last two decades, smart foods have played a major role thanks to their ability to protect the body and keep it functioning properly. Although "Smart Food" is not strictly a medical term, authoritative institutions have been using it for some time.

For example, the European Institute of Oncology has published a list of smart foods, divided according to the nutrients they contain. For instance, radicchio and pistachios are excellent sources of iron; nuts and soy oil are rich in omega-3 fatty acids; blackcurrants and kiwi in vitamin C; puffed rice and spinach in folates; almonds and rocket in calcium; while brown rice and raspberries serve to replenish fibre reserves.

Although scientific research has not been able to fully explain how these foods act in our bodies, many studies show that the consumption of foods with antioxidant properties is linked to a decline in the incidence of many diseases.

These foods essentially have two types of beneficial effects. On the one hand, the bionutrients contained in smart foods have high antioxidant capacity, contributing to the longevity of the cells. The oxidation processes caused by dreaded free radicals are often the cause of many diseases, including cancer and cardiovascular diseases. Therefore, the consumption of foods that inhibit or slow down the oxidation of cells, play a key role in protecting the body from the effects of aging.

On the other hand, choosing to eat these foods affects the relationship between nutrients and genetics. What we ingest provides information to our genes, thereby affecting the proteins that genes produce and, consequently, the way in which the body develops. For example, omega-3 fatty acids found in fish are essential for increasing brain plasticity and improving memory and learning.

Diets with a low omega-3 intake are associated with a higher risk of mental disorders, including dementia, dyslexia and bipolar syndrome, while diets rich in these nutrients "lubricate" the synapses, helping to improve cognitive abilities. These aspects are examined in nutrigenomics and nutrigenetics, sciences which aim to develop, in the not too distant future, personalised diets based on the genetic profile of the individual.

Going into a bit more detail, research on the healing and preventative powers of food has identified at least three major areas in which smart foods can exert their beneficial effects: in the prevention of diseases caused by diet, such as diabetes; in the prevention of neurodegenerative diseases and, in general, of cognitive decline associated with aging; in the prevention of cancer. In reality, these distinctions are not that rigid, because foods which keep the heart healthy also have a positive effect on the brain; moreover, the risk of cardiovascular disease is often associated with cognitive decline.

According to the American Institute for Cancer Research and the World Cancer Research Fund International, 30-40% of the most common cancers are preventable through a nutritious diet, maintaining a healthy weight and regular physical activity. Fruit and vegetables are among the foods which have the most effective cancer-protective action, especially when eaten raw. Therefore carrots, tomatoes, garlic, onions, shallots, but also broccoli, cabbage and Brussels sprouts. Some research indicates that the consumption of vegetables is associated with a reduced risk of colon cancer, while that of raw vegetables, especially carrots, leads to a lower incidence of breast cancer. Many fruits are rich in various nutrients, including isoflavones, lutein, beta-carotene, vitamin E and flavonoids, the combined action of which could explain their cancer-protective action.

As for aging and the neurodegenerative diseases that accompany it, antioxidants play a major role. Laboratory studies have established that a diet rich in spinach, vitamin E and strawberries can significantly slow down the symptoms of aging in rats. Therefore, the high antioxidant capacity of these foods could protect the central nervous system and thereby counteract cognitive decline in humans. Other research indicates that the consumption of cruciferous vegetables and green leafy vegetables is associated with a slower rate of cognitive decline women. Curcumin and vitamin E can potentially counteract the negative effect of diets that are high in trans and saturated fats. The flavonoids found in fruits, cocoa, beans, and ginkgo have a more complex mechanism of action in the human body, which is not yet fully understood. Blueberries improve memory and motor skills, counteracting the effect of aging on balance and coordination. Red wine, or better yet grape juice, has a similar effect on short-term memory and motor skills. Cocoa is also rich in antioxidants which can protect brain cells from oxidative stress that can promote the development of neurodegenerative diseases like Alzheimer's. Almonds and walnuts have the ability to reduce the risk of heart disease in women, while extra-virgin olive oil can lower blood pressure and cholesterol levels.

Although the study of bionutrients and their beneficial effect on the body is in its early stages, it is clear that a diet with the right amount of calories, rich in foods with antioxidant properties, is crucial for maintaining long term health.

This volume, filled with photographs and detailed descriptions, will take you on a journey in discovery of smart food, providing tasty and simple recipes complete with information on the seasonality of the foods, nutritional characteristics and the best cooking methods. The four sections - Breakfast, Starters, Mains, Juices and Smoothies - will give you the opportunity to eat healthily at any time of the day, tantalising your taste buds while helping your body to stay young for longer. However, this book is also designed to stress the importance of greater nutritional awareness, not only once the food is on the table, but from the moment it is bought. It is important, for example, to pay attention to labels and buy fresh fruits and vegetables, preferably seasonal. In short, the "smart" system doesn't just provide you with a list of foods; it is a holistic approach to nutrition that you can no longer live without!

Smart Cooking

It's not enough to choose the right foods; it is also important to dedicate the necessary attention, time and resources to meals. Unfortunately, organic products that are in harmony with nature cost a lot, and consequently a healthy diet is certainly more expensive, but our body is smart: if we eat the right foods, according to the season, we can eat less while feeling more sated and more energetic.

It is also true that reducing the amount of food we eat is our best resource for staying fit for longer. Many of today's problems are in fact determined by an excess amount of food, offered in various forms and with more innovative and seductive flavours for our palate and eyes. Although nature offers us many vegetables and fruits that we can use immediately, rich in nutrients that are perfect for the season, temperature and latitude, it is obviously unthinkable to reduce meal times to just a portion of simply washed fruit or vegetables. However, from nature we can learn that the more natural foods are, the more they are able to interact with our body. It is therefore worth replacing at least one meal a day with a "smart" meal of fresh raw or cooked organic foods.

What does changing diet mean? What cooking methods are used? Are the flavours very different? You need to keep in mind the fact that taste is "constructed": flavours are accepted if they are recognisable and refused if new. Smart cooking is very simple and instantaneous. Obviously you need to distance yourself from habits rooted in family traditions, but steaming is really easy, serving cooked food and raw food together is fun and colorful, and most importantly ... your health will improve!

BLOOD ORANGES

It is well known that oranges are an essential citrus fruit in our diet in winter, but their color makes a difference: Blood oranges are useful in the prevention of cardiovascular diseases. It seems that they are able to reduce and prevent the accumulation of fat. This is thanks to the anthocyanins, substances that also protect against tumours, diabetes and arteriosclerosis. Fresh in segments, juices or salads, oranges are a wonderful fruit to make full use of from autumn to late winter.

RASPBERRIES

This small berry - a concentrate of virtue and flavour - contains ellagic acid, a polyphenol antioxidant able to inhibit the metabolic processes that lead to the formation of cancer cells. Raspberries, which ripen between late spring and summer, are slightly laxative, useful for reducing stomach acid, and contain vitamin C, folic acid and retinol. As well as being beneficial when eaten fresh, this fruit, which is low in calories and rich in dietary fibre, does not lose its protective properties during cooking.

Anthocyanins are also the smart molecules in cherries, and the darker and more intense the red is, verging on black, the higher the concentration in the fruit! These fruit are recommended for diets, in order to improve disorders related to gout. Laboratory research has also revealed that the phenols in cherries are able to slow down cell proliferation. The fruit, which ripens from late spring to early summer, is mildly laxative, diuretic and low in calories: just 38 calories per 100 grams.

In Japan, the Persimmon tree is considered a symbol of peace because it survived the atomic bombing of Nagasaki, and now research has placed it among smart foods. Thanks to the fisetin, they counteract inflammation of the tissues, the carotenoids support the immune system, while the fibres have a beneficial effect on the digestive system. This autumn fruit is also rich in iron, phosphorus, vitamin C and retinol. As the retinol it fat-soluble, it is important to serve the fruit with fats, such as dried fruit or yogurt.

PERSIMMONS

CHERRIES

STRAWBERRIES

This is another example of anthocyanins together with the bright color of fruits that are actually inflorescences. Whatever they are, strawberries are low in calories, flavourful and rich in molecules that boost longevity. Fisetin and anthocyanins have a positive effect on diabetes, obesity, cancer and cardiovascular problems. Strawberries help lower "bad" cholesterol, reduce inflammation and are able to induce apoptosis in malignant cells, i.e. programmed cell death. They ripen in late spring.

APPLES

There are many different grades, colors and sizes of apples. They are rich in quercetin, a substance that has a protective function against stomach and intestinal cancer and which is able to prevent cells being attacked by cancer-causing substances. Furthermore, the fisetin – a flavonoid that is also present in fruits such as strawberries and persimmons – seems to reduce the feeling of hunger. Thanks to the pectin, mainly concentrated in the peel, apples improve digestion and stimulate intestinal peristalsis. This fruit is high in fibre, low calorie and rich in minerals and vitamins, making it a remarkable food source. They ripen between late summer and autumn, but you can find them all year.

PLUMS

CURRANTS

Red, black or white, these small clusters are without a doubt a valuable ally against inflammation. As with all the other berries, the anthocyanins (mainly present in blackcurrants) are beneficial to our well-being. Able to help in maintaining cardiovascular health, currants, like blueberries, can improve the elasticity of capillaries, veins and arteries. And we mustn't forget their high vitamin C content. Great for smoothies, juices and jams, they ripen between late spring and summer.

Blueberries help to keep your body in shape. One of their many properties is the ability to interact with the immune system, enhancing its function. But that's not all: the high vitamin C content makes them perfect natural antioxidants. Furthermore, thanks to the anthocyanins, they are believed to be an anticancer food when eaten in season and, above all, fresh. Despite being available year-round thanks to greenhouse cultivation, summer is the best time to reap all the benefits the fruit has to offer.

BLUEBERRIES

Plums, which come in different varieties and shapes, help digestion, have a laxative effect, promote the elimination of uric acid and, above all, blue or purple/black plums are rich in anthocyanins which, in addition to determining the color, are powerful antioxidants. Fresh plums have a higher water content and are lower in calories (42 calories per 100 grams) than dried ones, which concentrate the sugars and nutrients and have 230 calories per 100 grams. They ripen in summer and start growing in autumn.

GRAPES

Despite grapes being rich in sugars, they are fairly low calorie: 61 per 100 grams. Many people have the habit of peeling grapes and removing the seeds, but it is actually recommended that you eat them whole without discarding anything, as only in this way are they a balanced food that is able to detoxify and regulate intestinal functions. Furthermore, its polyphenols, resveratrol in particular, protect the body against cardiovascular diseases. They ripen between summer and autumn. There are also dried grapes on the market, but they are high calorie: 280 calories per 100 grams.

The fact that cabbage is a protective food has been reiterated for years and is recommended in the diets of both adults and children. In "red cabbage", or *Brassica oleracea var. capitata rubra*, in addition to the typical compounds present in cabbage, there are numerous anthocyanins in the pigments responsible for its beautiful color. Anthocyanins are considered a natural antidote to aging, as well as combatting free radicals and protecting against carcinogens. The more or less intense color is related to the pH of the soil where it is grown. In ripens in autumn.

RED CABBAGE

ONIONS

Once overcoming the problem of its pungent odour, the onion is one of the best allies to our health. It is rich in compounds that act in protecting the lungs and digestive tract, and is it also has detoxifying and purifying properties. And that's not all. Research has identified the "smart" molecule in the quercetin, which has a positive influence on the cardiovascular system. It is best eaten raw, in salads or crudités, because many of the compounds are lost during cooking. The yellow onion has a stronger flavour, while the red / purple one is sweeter and rich in anthocyanins.

This bud, which we often see sold in salt or oil, contains quercetin, a defender of our health; but not the only one! Perfect for flavouring sauces, entrées, starters and main courses, capers stimulate the appetite and digestive functions and help to reduce water retention. Moreover, thanks to the quercetin, it has anti-cancer properties and protective properties against inflammatory joint disease. It is an excellent natural supplement of vitamin A, C, E, K and B vitamins, and minerals like calcium, potassium and magnesium, to name but a few.

CAPERS

ASPARAGUS

Appreciated for their diuretic and purifying properties, asparagus are rich in fibre, vitamin C, vitamin K and carotenoids. But the "smart" substance is quercetin, which in addition to reducing the risk of breast, bowel and stomach cancers, protects vitamins C and E against free radicals. Rich in water and low in calories, the "shoots" (the edible part) are a spring vegetable. The best way to reap the benefits is to steam them and then season with extra virgin olive oil.

The sunny yellow color of the powder
obtained from the rhizomes of *Curcuma longa*
are an invitation to brighten up everyday
recipes. In fact, the constant
use of this spice is a good
way to help you live
to 100 years old, and
still be good shape!
Curcumin, the "smart"
substance found in
turmeric, improves
inflammatory
conditions and
reduces the
incidence of
osteoporosis,
Alzheimer's
and cancer. In
India, turmeric
is considered a
sacred spice and
is administered as a
medicine in Ayurvedic
medicine. It has a pleasant
taste and is one of the basic
ingredients for an excellent curry.

TURMERIC

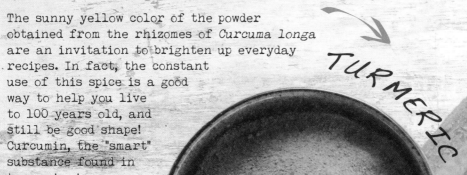

LETTUCE

Made up of over 94% water,
lettuce contains just 19
calories per 100 grams,
although it contains
large amounts of retinol,
folic acid and dietary
fibre. Research has
also shown that the
quercetin present
in lettuce (of which
over 150 varieties
are grown around the
world!) is able to act
positively in cases of
obesity and related
problems. In the United
States, salad is often
offered as a starter
because it reduces feelings
of hunger and is therefore
very useful in weight loss
diets and weight control. In
nature they ripen between the
beginning of spring and autumn.

They are diuretic, low in calories, useful
for liver function and rich in water and
dietary fibre. The skin, which should never
be removed, contains anthocyanins that give
aubergines their blue-purple or nearly black
color. They belong to the nightshade family
along with peppers, tomatoes and potatoes,
and are a summer vegetable par excellence.
The polyphenol content in aubergines
is an extraordinary defender of our
health and they are therefore
much welcomed to the table!
Before cooking, after being
sliced, you must sprinkle them
with salt to make them more
digestible.

AUBERGINES

CHILI PEPPER

Loved, trusted and appreciated,
the chili pepper is now found in
the pantries of most kitchens
in the world. For some it is an
everyday condiment, for others it's
just too hot, but its properties are
undeniable. The capsaicin it contains
is considered a "smart" molecule and
therefore able to increase lifespan!
But that's not all: it seems that the chili
pepper is also able to bypass thermoreceptors
and confuse neurons. It also reduces "bad"
cholesterol and increases the feeling of fullness,
thereby decreasing the amount of calories consumed.
It contains lots of vitamin C, folic acid and retinol, making
it a pillar of well-being.

GUINEA FOWL

This barnyard animal with an exotic history is native to North Africa (Numidia at the time of the Roman Empire). Its tasty white meat, more digestible than veal, is reminiscent of chicken, turkey and even pheasant, creating a delicious mixture of flavours. High protein and fairly lean (the fatty acids are concentrated mainly in the skin), it lends itself to various different preparations, but the best by far is roast guinea fowl. It has approximately 107 calories per 100 grams of lean meat.

TURKEY

Native to the Americas, the turkey is a barnyard bird that was introduced to Europe in the 1500s. Since then it has gladdened meals with its delicious lean, low cholesterol meat. Paramount to weight loss diets, it can also be found in the form of sausages, either sliced or whole. Naturally, to enjoy the health benefits of this meat it is best to choose a free-range, organic turkey.

Small fish rich in vitamin D, folic acid, retinol, niacin and minerals such as phosphorus, iron, calcium, sodium and potassium. Thanks to the presence of omega-3, they protect the heart and circulatory system, and are extremely beneficial in cases of hypertriglyceridemia. Often overlooked – perhaps because preparing dishes with this tiny blue fish is extremely time consuming – sardines are also good for the brain. It also appears that the humble and cheap sardine is able to protect important neurons from degeneration or death. They are great grilled, baked with herbs or marinated with lemon.

SARDINES

It belongs to the Salmonid family and in the wild it lives in cold water with strong currents or alpine lakes. It contains numerous proteins, is rich in omega-3 fatty acids, has a relatively low cholesterol content and contains significant amounts of minerals (for example, phosphorus) and vitamin D. The fact that it is low calorie (86 calories per 100 grams) makes it an excellent resource. Often overlooked, freshwater fish actually have some very interesting properties: it appears that trout flesh is also able to help the body eliminate excess toxins.

BROWN TROUT

HONEY

Honey is energy-boosting, nourishing, soothing, detoxifying for the liver, digestible and assimilable, as well as an excellent natural anti-inflammatory. It has several properties, depending on the flowers of origin: chestnut is anti-anaemia, eucalyptus and lime have an anti-inflammatory effect on airways, the strawberry tree is diuretic, thyme is antiseptic and rhododendron can help people suffering from insomnia. Honey has always been considered a "food-medicine" and continues to be recommended for its anti-cancer properties. It contains 303 calories per 100 grams.

WHOLE MILK YOGURT

Yogurt is a "pre-digested" food. It is actually milk that has been turned into an easily digestible fermented product by the bacteria *Lactobacillus bulgaricus* and *Streptococcus thermophilus*, and it provides several benefits to the digestive system. Eating yogurt regularly strengthens the immune system and in winter it is a great help in fighting off colds. It also improves water absorption, so consuming yogurt and water together is ideal for helping your body rehydrate after exercise.

Eggs are not just food, they are also a condiment and basic ingredient for many recipes, and are rich in nutrients (they have them all: just sugars are missing!). As many people prefer to use just the egg yolk or egg white, it is good to know that the yolk, if eaten raw, is able to improve liver and gallbladder functions, while egg white is good for anaemia because it raises the level of albumin in the blood. A whole egg is certainly balanced, but only when cooked in the right way: ideally it should be soft-boiled or poached.

CHICKEN EGGS

GOAT'S MILK

As we age, the body produces less lactase and therefore milk becomes harder to digest. Goat's milk is one of the most assimilable, but, like cow's milk, is not suitable for those with intolerances or allergies to animal milk. For those who consume it regularly, it is important to know that it has 72 calories per 100 grams and contains calcium, sodium, potassium, phosphorus, zinc and vitamins such as retinol. The cholesterol intake is lower than cow's milk and it is perfect for making smoothies and snacks. It is particularly suitable for sportspersons, students and children.

GARLIC

Many people don't like garlic because it makes the breath smell bad, but allicin (responsible for the characteristic appetising aroma that is released when it is just cut or crushed) appears to be the substance that protects against stomach cancer. The bulb also helps boost the immune system. It's ideal eaten raw, in salads, finely grated or crushed with a pestle for preparing soups, condiments and sauces. It seems that the odour decreases if eaten regularly, but this is nothing compared to the health benefits that garlic offers us.

BROCCOLI

Broccoli is low in calories and the high water and fibre content contributes to healthier intestinal flora. However, it is vitamin C (crucial to combat cardiovascular disease) that makes the difference: 100 grams of broccoli accounts for half of our daily requirement. Moreover, it seems that broccoli has anti-cancer properties and protects the lungs and colon. A typical autumn and winter vegetable, broccoli is great raw in crudités or, to make it more easily digestible, lightly steamed.

It stimulates digestion, relieves stomach cramps and is a valuable ally against halitosis, but above all its delicious aroma improves our perception of the flavours to which it is associated. It contains iron, calcium, phosphorus, sodium and potassium, as well as vitamin C, folic acid and retinol. This annual aromatic plant is typically used to enhance summer dishes, such as salads with tomatoes, onions and cucumbers. A useful piece of information for those who have lactose intolerance and need a source of calcium: 10 grams of basil corresponds to a large glass of milk!

BASIL

PARSLEY

An aromatic plant that is essential in the kitchen, but also for our health. In addition to improving the taste of many foods (vegetables, meat, fish and cereals), parsley is a source of the valuable quercetin, a flavonoid that protects vitamins C and E. Parsley is purifying and diuretic, it stimulates the appetite, contains high amounts of retinol, dietary fibre, calcium, iron, phosphorus and potassium, and is low calorie.

GREEN TEA

It is considered an anti-cancer drink par excellence; the most powerful anti-free radicals for quenching your thirst. The molecule that green tea provides to reduce, or even eliminate, the free radicals that lead to aging and tissue oxidation is called "Epigallocatechin Gallate", abbreviated to EGCG. But that's not all EGCG does: it seems that it is also able to trigger the death of cancer cells. It's best to drink it plain, without sweeteners.

RADICCHIO

A member of the Chicory family, radicchio is a slightly bitter leaf with purple hues that can be identified as: Treviso, Castelfranco, Verona or Chioggia. Rich in water, fibre, minerals and vitamins, with just 13 calories per 100 grams, radicchio is excellent in winter! It is "smart" thanks to anthocyanins, which give it the typical dark red hues. Fresh and crisp, it is great to serve raw in salads. You can reduce the bitterness (for those who don't like it) by adding onions or carrots. It ripens in autumn and winter.

The quercetin present in cocoa means that you can eat it quite happily; even better, with the knowledge that this gluttonous food is actually able to counteract damage caused by aging. But chocolate, especially dark chocolate, is also a valuable aid for regulating blood pressure and reducing "bad" cholesterol. The downside is the high-caloric content (542 calories per 100 grams). According to experts, however, as long as you stay within the limit of 20-30 grams per day, chocolate improves mood and general well-being!

They look great and when steamed the color remains almost unchanged thanks to the anthocyanins. Anthocyanins, which belong to the flavonoid family, are water soluble and in plants have the function to protect them from drought and damage caused by ultraviolet radiation. Purple potatoes are able to counteract tissue oxidation and the aging processes. High in calories (84 calories per 100 grams), they are a great substitute for other carbohydrates, as long as they are eaten boiled or steamed. They ripen in the summer, but can be easily preserved throughout the year.

TOMATOES

The lycopene in tomatoes has anti-cancer properties and protects the pancreas, ovaries and prostate. Although delicious in summer eaten raw in salads, juices or on bruschetta, it is equally important to eat tomatoes in winter, cooking them to make sauces for cereals or cooked vegetables. Tomatoes don't like the cold and if you keep in the refrigerator they will lose much of their aroma; it is therefore best to keep them in a cool, dry place, even hanging in bunches.

OAT

Replacing whole wheat flour, pasta and bread with that of other cereals can only bring enormous benefits to your health, and it's even better if you substitute flours with seeds. A seed is in fact a complete microcosm, perfect, able to germinate and create new life; unlike flour, which "dies" just a few days after grinding and is often processed so that it can be preserved longer. Oat groats are high protein, contain lipids, minerals and vitamins, and help improve digestion thanks to the fibres.

Better in flour or grains?
Both are good, but the flour
must be fresh and without
the addition of other
ingredients, while the
grains are perfect for
salads, minestrones and
soups. Thanks to the fibres
and proteins, spelt is a
good ally in weight loss
diets as it helps reach
a pleasant feeling of
fullness, with smaller
quantities. It stimulates
the immune system, aids
digestion and is useful for
relieving abdominal bloating
and cramps. It also appears to
improve blood circulation and
tissue oxygenation.

SPELT

WHOLE GRAIN WHEAT

Mainly present on our
tables in its refined
form (bread, pasta, bread
sticks, creams, cakes,
biscuits), perhaps far
too much. It is in fact
better to eat whole
wheat, as it "integrates"
our diet and provides
nutrients necessary to
our well-being. In contrast,
refined wheat is actually
useless, if not harmful. Wheat is
an excellent food to associate with other cereals.
It is nutritious, high protein and energy boosting,
containing 319 calories per 100 grams.

It belongs to the Chenopodiaceae family and comes from the Andes, apparently taking energy, strength and an abundance of minerals from these mountains! The high protein content makes quinoa an excellent alternative to traditional cereals, and being gluten-free it is suitable for those suffering from celiac disease. Rich in fibre, it is indicated for those with digestive problems. It has fat burning properties and is a valuable aid in weight loss diets thank to its high satiating power. It contains lysine, which stimulates the production of serotonin, a neurotransmitter linked to good mood states!

QUINOA

BUCKWHEAT

Buckwheat is an annual herbaceous plant belonging to the Polygonaceae family and its seeds are rich in lysine and tryptophan. They do not however contain gluten. The flour is ideal for preparing very tasty homemade bread and pasta; the groats are great for soups and salads. For mountain populations it is symbolic of strength due to its ability to grow in inaccessible areas with a cold climate. In Italy today, it is mainly used to make regional types of pasta (for example, pizzoccheri) or Polenta Taragna.

BARLEY

Barley is highly digestible and helps to accelerate gastrointestinal transit, so it can be used to regulate and detoxify the digestive system. Unfortunately barley isn't used nearly enough, even if thanks to its soluble fibre (beta-glucans) it is able to reduce "bad" cholesterol. A great wheat substitute, it also seems to be beneficial for cardiovascular problems and can help prevent breast cancer.

WHOLE GRAIN RICE

Whole grain rice has many benefits. A source of minerals, vitamins and essential amino acids, it is a staple food for vegans and vegetarians. It is recommended for those suffering from celiac disease or gluten intolerance, and is able to restore digestive functions. It is easily digestible, helps regulate sugar levels in the blood, reduces "bad" cholesterol and is highly satiating. Macrobiotics, which considers it a staple food for a healthy and balanced body, recommends chewing it for a long time to promote lymphatic circulation.

Thanks to the high fibre content, this rice is recommended for maintaining healthy intestinal flora. It has a low glycemic index and is therefore indicated for weight loss diets. Its color indicates the presence of anthocyanin, a flavonoid that protects against free radicals and thereby slows down the natural aging process.

BLACK VENERE RICE

EXTRA VIRGIN OLIVE OIL

A condiment par excellence. Although extra virgin olive oil is extremely high calorie (900 calories per 100 grams!), it is important to include it in our diet - especially uncooked - in order to improve the absorption of fat-soluble vitamins and digestibility of foods, to lubricate the digestive system and support the cardiovascular system. Furthermore, it conteracts "bad" cholesterol and the formation of gallbladder stones, as well as strengthening the immune system. Recent studies have demonstrated the presence of oleocanthal, a compound similar to a pain killer that also seems to have anti-cancer properties.

Sunflower seed oil is the perfect alternative for those who dislike the intense flavour of extra virgin olive oil, although it must be cold pressed and organic; two characteristics which make the difference. However, we recommend that you to eliminate or gradually reduce deep-fried and fried foods from your diet, and that you add this condiment to food after cooking. Sunflower seed oil should be kept in a dark, cool place, as it deteriorates easily. It's also better to choose glass bottles or cans rather than plastic, in order to prevent contamination or deterioration of the product.

COLD PRESSED SUNFLOWER SEED OIL

WALNUTS

There are 654 calories in 100 grams of walnuts, but the ideal daily amount is 5-6 nuts. Rich in omega-3, they are especially suitable for those who don't like fats in general and consume little fish or meat. They should be part of everyone's diet, because the polyunsaturated acids they contain are good for the heart and circulatory system. A source of calcium, phosphorus, zinc and iron, walnuts are a natural supplement that can also reduce "bad" cholesterol.

ALMONDS

Very high calorie (540 calories per 100 grams), but a dozen with cereal and yogurt are enough for a surprisingly complete and light breakfast. It also appears that the dry nuts can protect against some cancers, such as colon cancer and pancreatic cancer. Extremely energy-boosting and high in protein, they are indicated for vegetarian and vegan diets, as well as for all those who don't like animal fats and want to eliminate cheese and milk, because they are a source of essential calcium, minerals and vitamins.

SOY

Research has shown that in countries where soy is part of the daily diet, the incidence of colon cancer is less than in countries where animal-based proteins are predominant. Soy is an important source of protein (36%); furthermore, the proteins it contains are rich in essential amino acids, i.e. those that the body is unable to synthesise on its own. Soy helps lower bad cholesterol, prevents osteoporosis and is beneficial for menopausal disorders. Soy can be found in the form of tofu, milk, oil, tamari, sprouts, steaks, seeds and jam.

These are tiny berries similar to blueberries, just as rich in anthocyanins, and in North America (place of origin) they are considered one of the most antioxidant rich foods. Regular consumption of Aronia berries seems to help the body fight infections and prevent the premature aging of cells. Aronia berries are rich in vitamins A, C, E and K. The berries are also a good source of fibre and thereby contribute to improving digestive functions. You can find them dried, in the form of juice or in jams.

If you have a small vegetable garden, planting this variety of beans is a wonderful experience. They are delicious when the seed is unripe and the pod looks tender and crunchy, and they promote diuresis, improve digestive function thanks to the fibres and, as they are low calorie, are ideal in weight loss diets. When the seeds are ripe the pod dries out to reveal dark blue beans, which indicates the presence of anthocyanins. Excellent substitutes for animal protein, they are an important source of B vitamins (B1, B2 and B3), which are essential for the metabolism of sugars, cell development and to counteract cholesterol.

Breakfast...

It is well-known that breakfast is the most important meal of the day. The calories eaten in the morning - which should correspond to a fifth of the daily requirement - are fundamental: on the one hand, they help us to maintain a healthy weight; on the other hand, they give us enough energy for the day ahead. But eating breakfast is not enough: we must pay attention to the quality of the foods we eat. It is quality foods that optimise energy levels, helping us to avoid drowsiness related to the digestion of heavy foods.

The recipes in this section contain all the essential ingredients for a balanced breakfast. Yogurt, for example, contains protein and fibre, and has a low glycemic index. You'll feel full for longer, without the danger of your blood sugar dropping suddenly. Nuts are ideal sources of "friendly" fats - the famous omega-3 (monounsaturated) and omega-9 (polyunsaturated) fatty acids - while chocolate is jam-packed with antioxidants ... but don't overdo it!

Energy Bars with Cereal and Nuts

Servings

3 1/2 cups (200 g) cereal flakes (oats, barley and wheat) – 1/4 cup (30 g) sesame seeds – 2 tbsp (about 50 g) honey – 2 tbsp (30 g) soy butter – 1/4 cup (20 g) almonds – 1/4 cup (20 g) hazelnuts – 2 tbsp (20 g) soaked raisins

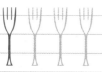

Difficulty

Prep Time
10 minutes

Cooking Time
20 minutes

1. Pour 2 tbsp (15 g) of sesame seeds onto a sheet of parchment paper.

2. Combine the honey and the butter in a saucepan and heat until you have a uniform mixture. Add all the other ingredients a little at a time until the mixture becomes too dense to stir. Transfer onto the sheet coated with sesame seeds.

3. Distribute the rest of the sesame seeds on top and even out the surface with your hands. Cover with another sheet of parchment paper and thin out until you have a sheet 1/2 in. (1 cm) thick.

4. After having preheated the oven to 390 degrees F (200 degrees C), cut the mixture into bars of desired size and set on the baking sheet. Bake for about 20 minutes then take out of the oven and allow to cool before serving.

Purple Rice Cookies with Berries

For the cookies: 3/4 cup (120 g) Venere rice flour – 1/4 cup (30 g) whole wheat flour – 5 tbsp (about 50 g) cold-pressed corn oil – 5 tbsp (about 50 g) honey – 1 egg
For the cream: 1 2/3 cups (4 dl) oat milk – 1 1/2 tbsp (15 g) Venere rice flour – 1/3 cup (50 g) blueberries – 1/3 cup (50 g) currants – 1/3 cup (50 g) strawberries – 6 romanesco broccoli florets – 1 organic lemon – fresh mint to taste

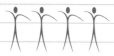

Servings

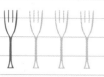

Difficulty

Prep Time
30 minutes

Resting Time
30 minutes

Cooking Time
15 minutes

1. Preheat the oven to 390 degrees F (200 degrees C). Mix all the cookie ingredients until the mixture is supple and homogeneous. Cool in the refrigerator for 20 minutes then roll out to a thickness of about 1/16 in. (2 mm).

2. Cut out the cookies using a cookie cutter of the desired shape and set on a baking sheet lined with parchment paper. Bake for 15 minutes, take out of the oven and set on the countertop to cool.

3. Trim all the fruit, mint and cauliflower. Right before making breakfast, pour the oat milk into a saucepan. Incorporate the flour and cook over low heat until the mixture thickens slightly. Last, add a few drops of freshly squeezed lemon juice, boil for a few minutes and pour into cups.

4. Allow to cool and serve with fruit, cauliflower, lemon slices and mint to taste. Accompany with the Venere rice cookies.

Chestnut Flour Rustic Cookies

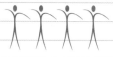

Servings

1 2/3 cups (150 g) chestnut flour - 3/4 cups (100 g) semi whole wheat flour - 1 egg - 5 tbsp (about 50 g) sunflower oil - 1/4 cup (0.5 dl) milk - 2 1/2 tbsp (30 g) sugar

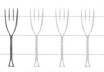

Difficulty

1. Preheat the oven to 390 degrees F (200 degrees C).

2. Combine and knead all the ingredients together. Once you have a homogeneous dough, shape on a sheet of parchment paper until the dough is compact (possibly long rather than wide) and about 1-1.5 in. (3-4 cm) thick.

3. Bake for 30 minutes then take out of the oven and slice into cookies about 1/2-3/4 in. (1-2 cm) wide.

4. Allow to cool: these rustic cookies, which are soft upon cutting, will harden when cooled. Perfect for dipping in milk, wine or cream, they are an excellent energetic and flavorful snack!

Prep Time
20 minutes

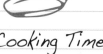

Cooking Time
30 minutes

Dark Chocolate Pudding

Servings

1/3 cup (40 g) unsweetened cocoa powder – 1 tbsp (10 g) cornstarch – 1 2/3 cups (4 dl) goat milk – 2 tbsp (about 24 g) brown sugar – 1/2 cup (1 dl) water – 1 tbsp (about 3 g) grated lemon zest – 1 tbsp (about 2 g) grated ginger – 1 tbsp (9 g) raisins

Difficulty

1. In a bowl, blend the sugar, cocoa powder and starch with a whisk (to avoid the formation of clumps) then drizzle in and incorporate water and milk. Last, add the lemon zest and ginger.

2. Transfer the mixture into a steel saucepan and bring to a boil stirring continuously over very low heat.

**Prep Time
5 minutes**

3. After about 2 minutes of boiling, the mixture will begin to thicken. Take off the heat, pour into molds and decorate with the raisins.

4. Place in the fridge to cool before serving.

**Resting Time
1 hour**

**Cooking Time
5 minutes**

Fruit Preserves with Multi Cereal Bread

Servings

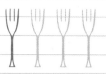

Difficulty

Prep Time
6 minutes

Cooking Time
100 minutes

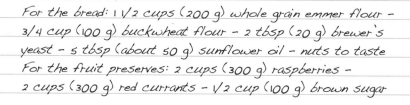

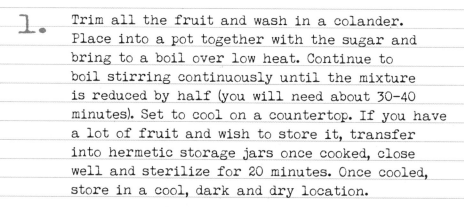

For the bread: 1 1/2 cups (200 g) whole grain emmer flour – 3/4 cup (100 g) buckwheat flour – 2 tbsp (20 g) brewer's yeast – 5 tbsp (about 50 g) sunflower oil – nuts to taste
For the fruit preserves: 2 cups (300 g) raspberries – 2 cups (300 g) red currants – 1/2 cup (100 g) brown sugar

1. Trim all the fruit and wash in a colander. Place into a pot together with the sugar and bring to a boil over low heat. Continue to boil stirring continuously until the mixture is reduced by half (you will need about 30-40 minutes). Set to cool on a countertop. If you have a lot of fruit and wish to store it, transfer into hermetic storage jars once cooked, close well and sterilize for 20 minutes. Once cooled, store in a cool, dark and dry location.

2. Pour the flours into a bowl and mix well with a fork. Dissolve the yeast in 3/4 cup (200 g) of lukewarm water. Add it to the flours along with half of the oil and mix again until the mixture is soft. If necessary, add some more water, a tablespoon at a time. Set the dough aside to rise in a warm location. If you have the time you can let it sit for as long as 24 hours.

3. Right before making the bread, preheat the oven to 350 degrees F (180 degrees C). Incorporate chopped nuts and using your hands coated in oil give the dough the shape you prefer for your bread. To add softness, overlay two sheets of dough, roll them up and set into a container.

4. Bake for 60 minutes but lower the temperature to 320 degrees F (160 degrees C) after the first 15 minutes. Once baked, set to cool on the countertop.

Green Tea Cream with Yogurt

Servings

1 cup (2.5 dl) milk – 1 tbsp (10 g) green tea powder –
2 1/2 tbsp (30 g) brown sugar – 3/4 cup (200 g) non dairy
cream – 3/4 cup (200 g) frozen soy yogurt

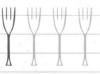

Difficulty

Prep Time
40 minutes

Resting Time
3 hours

Cooking Time
5 minutes

1. Bring the milk to a boil and dissolve the tea and the sugar. Take off the heat and allow to cool. Whip the cream and incorporate into the mixture.

2. Pour into an ice cream machine and churn for about 30 minutes. Store in the freezer until needed. If you don't have an ice cream machine, pour the mixture into a steel container and place in the freezer.

3. Take out every 20 minutes or so and stir. Repeat for about 3 hours.

4. Right before serving, combine the green tea ice cream with the frozen yogurt using a fork, to render it creamier. Compose the dessert by mixing the two flavors to taste.

White Rice Crêpes with Chocolate Hazelnut Cream

Servings

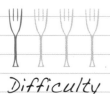

Difficulty

Prep Time
40 minutes

Cooking Time
20 minutes

For the crêpes: 1/3 cup (50 g) white rice flour – 1/2 cup (50 g) buckwheat flour – 1 1/4 cups (3 dl) milk – 2 eggs – 2 tbsp (about 20 g) sunflower oil
For the cream: 1/3 cup (100 g) hazelnut cream – 3.5 oz. (100 g) dark chocolate

1. First, prepare the filling. Place the hazelnut cream and chopped chocolate into a double boiler. Melt while stirring continuously. Once the cream is uniform, take off the heat and transfer into a bowl.

2. Pour the milk, eggs and flour into a different bowl. Whisk the mixture until it is fluid and clump free.

3. Grease a non-stick frying pan using a paper towel dipped in oil.

4. Place over heat and pour in the batter one ladleful at a time. Tilt and turn the frying pan until the batter covers the bottom in a thin and uniform layer. After about one minute, turn over. Leave over heat for a few more seconds then transfer onto a plate. Repeat until the batter is finished.

5. Fill the crêpes with the chocolate hazelnut cream and place in a hot oven for 2 minutes.

6. Serve hot or at room temperature with some cream on the side.

Whole Grain Apple and Nut Pockets

Servings

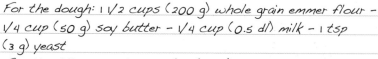

For the dough: 1 1/2 cups (200 g) whole grain emmer flour –
1/4 cup (50 g) soy butter – 1/4 cup (0.5 dl) milk – 1 tsp
(3 g) yeast
For the filling: 1 apple – 2 tbsp (20 g) raisins – 10 walnuts –
1 tbsp (about 15 g) honey – 10 walnut kernels for decoration

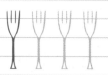

Difficulty

1. Mix the flour, butter, milk and yeast in a bowl.
Once the mixture is well blended, soft and clump
free, set aside to rest for 20 minutes.

2. Soak the raisins; wash and dice the apple; clean
the walnuts. Place all the filling ingredients
into a bowl and blend.

Prep Time
20 minutes

3. Preheat the oven to 350 degrees F (180 degrees C)
and line a baking sheet with waxed paper. Place
parchment paper on a comfortable working
surface and roll out the dough on top. After
rolling out evenly to a thickness of about 1/16
in. (2 mm), cut out circles. Place some filling
on half of the circles and cover with the rest.
Seal the edges well to make sure the filling
does not seep out when baked. Brush the surface
with honey.

Cooking Time
20 minutes

4. Bake the pockets for about 20 minutes then allow
to cool on the countertop. Brush the tops with
honey once more and decorate with the walnut
kernels.

Rice, Corn and Whole Wheat Flour Bread with Flavored Yogurt

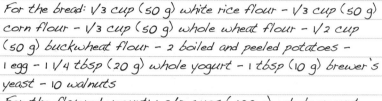

For the bread: 1/3 cup (50 g) white rice flour - 1/3 cup (50 g) corn flour - 1/3 cup (50 g) whole wheat flour - 1/2 cup (50 g) buckwheat flour - 2 boiled and peeled potatoes - 1 egg - 1 1/4 tbsp (20 g) whole yogurt - 1 tbsp (10 g) brewer's yeast - 10 walnuts

For the flavored yogurt: 1 2/3 cups (400 g) whole yogurt - 1 spring onion - 10 pitted olives - 4 small tomatoes - salt and pepper

Servings

Difficulty

Prep Time
30 minutes

Cooking Time
50 minutes

1. After preheating the oven to 350 degrees F (180 degrees C), mash the potatoes until they are creamy. Pour the flours, buckwheat, egg and yogurt into a bowl. Amalgamate with the potato puree, adding water and yeast (dissolved in a glass of warm water) to facilitate the process.

2. Continue kneading until the dough is homogeneous. If it becomes too hard or not very flexible, add water one tablespoon at a time. Once the dough is well-kneaded, set it aside to rest in a warm location for a couple of hours.

3. Divide the dough into buns, or form a rope or any other shape of your choice. Before placing into the oven, sprinkle with the hazelnuts. Bake for 50 minutes then check that the interior is done using a toothpick. Once out of the oven, allow to cool before serving.

4. Peel and slice the spring onion. Wash and chop the tomatoes. Finely chop the olives. Add the ingredients to the yogurt. Season with salt and pepper, and mix. Serve the resulting yogurt with slices of bread. It is a perfect summer breakfast!

Nut and Oat Bars

Servings

1/2 cup (30 g) oat flakes - 1/3 cup (50 g) hazelnut flour - 1/2 cup (50 g) almond flour - 2 tbsp (about 24 g) brown sugar - 1/4 cup (50 g) diced soy butter - 2 yolks

Difficulty

1. After preheating the oven to 390 degrees F (200 degrees C), blend all the ingredients and transfer onto a sheet of parchment paper. Continue to gently work the ingredients with your fingers to thin out the mixture and make it more compact.

Prep Time
10 minutes

2. Take another sheet of waxed paper and set it on top of the mixture. Roll a rolling pin over the mixture until it is about 1/16-1/8 in. (2-3 mm) thick. Transfer the rolled out mixture onto a baking sheet lined with parchment paper. Try to give it a regular shape but don't worry if it's not perfect, it will be cut into pieces later.

3. Bake for 15-20 minutes then transfer the finished product with the parchment paper onto a comfortable working surface. Cut into irregular pieces following your imagination and allow to cool. Once cooled, the bars are delightedly crunchy.

Cooking Time
20 minutes

Plum Cake

3/4 cup (100 g) whole wheat flour - 3/4 cup (100 g) buckwheat flour - 1/2 cup (50 g) oat flour - 2 eggs - 1/4 cup (50 g) brown sugar - 5 tbsp (about 50 g) sunflower oil - 1/2 cup (0.5 dl) goat milk - 1/2 tbsp (5 g) baking powder - 10 oz. (300 g) purple plums - 2 tbsp (about 20 g) sunflower oil and 2 tbsp (about 25 g) brown sugar for coating the baking sheet

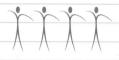

Servings

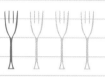

Difficulty

Prep Time
15 minutes

Cooking Time
40 minutes

1. Preheat the oven to 350 degrees F (180 degrees C) then oil a baking pan of your choice and coat in brown sugar. Wash the plums and cut them into halves, eliminating the pit.

2. Pour the flours into a bowl, blend with a fork and incorporate the rest of the ingredients one at a time until the mixture is soft, smooth and clump free.

3. Pour the batter into the baking pan, smooth out the surface and arrange the plums on top. Bake for 40 minutes. Every so often, check to make sure the plums are softening without burning and the cake is starting to rise.

4. Use a toothpick to check that the inside of the cake is cooked. If the toothpick comes out dry, you can take the dessert out of the oven. If not, leave in for an additional 10 minutes. Once out of the oven, allow to cool on the countertop.

Whole Grain Carrot Cake

Servings

1 1/2 cups (150 g) oat flour - 1/3 cup (50 g) whole wheat flour - 2 steamed carrots - 2 eggs - 1/4 cup (0.5 dl) goat milk - 5 tbsp (about 50 g) extra virgin olive oil - 3 tbsp (30 g) soaked chokeberries - 1/3 tbsp (3 g) baking powder - salt and pepper - 2 tbsp (about 20 g) extra virgin olive oil and 2 tbsp (16.5 g) sesame seeds for coating the molds

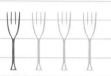

Difficulty

1. Preheat the oven to 350 degrees F (180 degrees C). Grease a baking pan or single serving molds with oil and coat with sesame seeds.

2. Blend the carrots with the milk in a blender. Pour the mixture into a bowl and incorporate sieved flours. Add the eggs, oil, salt, pepper and yeast. Once you have a smooth, clump free batter, add the chokeberries, well drained.

Prep Time
20 minutes

3. Transfer the batter into the baking pan and bake for 40 minutes. If the surface starts darkening too much during baking, cover with parchment paper.

4. Once cooked, take the cake or mini cakes out of the oven and cool before cutting. The cake is also excellent filled with cheese, ricotta, sliced tomatoes etc.

Cooking Time
40 minutes

Almond Yogurt with Berries and Apples

Servings

2 cups (500 g) almond yogurt - 3 1/2 cups (500 g) mixed berries - 1 sliced, dehydrated apple - 1 apple - 1 tbsp malt

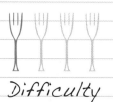

Difficulty

1. Wash, peel and chop the apple.

2. Trim the berries and place them into a saucepan along with the apple and the malt.

3. Cook over low heat until the fruit has disintegrated and amalgamated well. You will need about 30 minutes.

Prep Time
15 minutes

4. Set aside to cool.

5. Before serving, divide the yogurt between the diners, cover with cooked fruit and decorate with strips of dehydrated apples.

Cooking Time
30 minutes

If you want to prepare dehydrated apple strips at home, finely slice the apples (use a very sharp knife or a food slicer). Arrange the resulting slices on a baking sheet and bake for 2-3 hours at 122-140 degrees F (50-60 degrees C), or arrange on a non-stick frying pan and allow to dry over low, diffuse heat. Turn the slices over several times and in 10 minutes, they will be dehydrated.

Starters...

Starters deserve special attention because traditionally white or "refined" flours are used, but they have a high glycemic index. It is therefore best to use wholemeal flour and rice, and obviously pay attention to the quality of the other ingredients used and the size of the portions.

Chili peppers, garlic and curry are ideal for giving flavour to dishes and for their anti-inflammatory properties. The fibre contained in vegetables slows down the absorption of sugars and carbohydrates, thereby avoiding blood glucose spikes. We therefore suggest them often, both cooked and raw, as an accompaniment or sauce for our starters. Remember to choose "good" fats, such as olive oil, and try to replace ordinary cream with oat or soy cream to reduce the saturated fat content; they're just as tasty! Pistachios, walnuts or chopped almonds are invaluable ingredients and contribute to the daily intake of omega-3 and omega-9.

Chili Pepper Cream with Mixed Vegetables

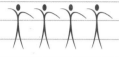

Servings

For the cream: 3/4 cup (200 g) yogurt similar to Greek –
3 tsp (5 g) paprika – 1 fresh chili pepper – 1 small spring
onion – 1 lime – salt and pepper
For the vegetables: 1 zucchini – 2 purple potatoes –
2 carrots – 1 eggplant – 2 tomatoes

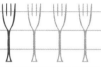

Difficulty

1. Wash and steam the zucchini, potatoes and carrots. Once they are soft (about 20-30 minutes later), transfer onto a plate.

2. Place the yogurt, paprika and sliced spring onion (including the unwilted green portion) into a bowl. Add freshly sliced chili pepper of desired spiciness. Dilute with lime juice then season with salt and pepper to taste.

Prep Time
10 minutes

3. Wash and slice the eggplant. Sprinkle with salt to draw out the juices then wash once more. Dry and briefly sauté on a grill or in a non-stick frying pan to soften. Wash and cut two tomatoes in half. Cook them next to the eggplants.

4. At service, accompany the vegetables with the cream. An excellent dish for hot summer days, it is perfect served at room temperature.

Cooking Time
30 minutes

Buckwheat and Trout Fillets in Herbs

Servings

2/3 cup (100 g) buckwheat - 4 trout fillets about 7 oz. (200 g) each - 20 basil leaves - 2 1/2 tbsp (20 g) breadcrumbs - 10 almonds - 4 tbsp (about 40 g) extra virgin olive oil - salt and pepper

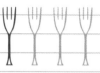

Difficulty

Prep Time
20 minutes

Cooking Time
40 minutes

1. Wash the buckwheat and boil covered for 30 minutes. Once cooked, leave in the water until needed.

2. Wash the trout fillets leaving them moist. Mince the basil leaves and finely chop the almonds. Combine them with the breadcrumbs and mix.

3. Coat the fillets in the breading applying gentle pressure to make sure it sticks to the meat well.

4. Pour the oil into a non-stick frying pan and cook the fish over medium heat. Turn the fillets over several times. Once they begin to release an aroma (about 3-4 minutes later).

5. Serve them accompanied with a portion of unseasoned buckwheat. It is an excellent substitute for bread or breadsticks. Season with salt and pepper before eating.

Lettuce and Cereal Salad

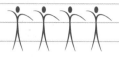

Servings

1/2 cup (100 g) cooked emmer – 2/3 cup (100 g) cooked barley – 1/2 cup (100 g) cooked oats – 2 organic oranges – 1 head of iceberg lettuce – 2 tbsp (20 g) raisins – 2 tbsp (20 g) chokeberries – 10 chopped walnut kernels – 1 minced dried chili pepper – 4 tbsp (about 40 g) extra virgin olive oil – salt

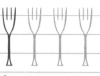

Difficulty

1. Soak the dried fruit in lukewarm water for 10 minutes then drain. Wash the oranges then peel one, doing your best to remove only the external oil-rich portion of the peel and not the pith (the white part). Slice the peel into small strips.

2. Wash and chop the head of lettuce (without taking it apart) and set aside to dry until needed. Finely slice the remaining orange and juice the peeled orange.

Prep Time
5 minutes

3. Place all the cereals into a bowl and add the dried fruit, the orange juice, slices and peel strips, and the lettuce. Season with oil, chili pepper and salt to taste.

4. Gently mix and serve immediately to ensure the lettuce remains fresh.

Cold Pasta Salad with Cabbage

Servings

10 oz. (300 g) whole wheat short pasta (fusilli, penne) –
3.5 oz. (100 g) purple cabbage – 3.5 oz. (100 g) green cabbage –
3.5 oz. (100 g) Romanesco broccoli florets – 3.5 oz. (100 g)
broccoli – 20 almonds – 10 capers in salt – 2 garlic cloves –
4 tbsp (about 40 g) extra virgin olive oil – salt and pepper

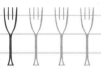

Difficulty

Prep Time
10 minutes

Cooking Time
10 minutes

1. Trim all the vegetables. Dry the purple and green cabbage well and slice removing the cores and any hard sections.

2. Chop the broccoli and Romanesco then peel and mince the garlic.

3. Irregularly chop the almonds and the capers, without rinsing away the salt.

4. Transfer all the vegetables into a bowl. Season with the oil, almonds, capers, salt and pepper.

5. Boil the pasta following the instructions on the packaging. Drain and add to the condiment.

6. Mix together and set aside for at least an hour before serving.

Orecchiette with Broccoli

Servings

2 1/3 cups (300 g) whole wheat flour – 2/3 cup (150 g)
water – 14 oz. (400 g) broccoli florets – 2 garlic cloves –
2 fresh chili peppers of desired spiciness – 1/4 cup (50 g)
oat cream – 4 tbsp extra virgin olive oil – salt

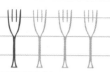

Difficulty

Prep Time
15 minutes

Cooking Time
30 minutes

1. Mix the flour with the water and knead until the dough is homogeneous. If necessary, add some water one tablespoon at a time.

2. Divide the dough into pieces and form ropes. Cut them into pieces about inches 1/8 in. (3 mm) wide and flatten them with your fingertips to give them the typical orecchiette shape. Set aside on a floured cloth until needed.

3. Wash the broccoli and chop. Peel the garlic and cut into halves. Wash and slice the chili peppers and add them to the garlic. Pour the oil into a wide frying pan and set over low heat. Add the chili pepper and garlic for some flavor. Next, add the broccoli and cook with the cover on for 5 minutes, mixing regularly. If you prefer your vegetables soft, cook for 5 more minutes, adding a few tablespoons of water. Season with salt once cooked.

4. Boil the orecchiette in salted water. Once they have the desired consistency, drain and add to the condiment. Add the cream and mix. Heat for about 1 minute and serve.

Corn Pasta with Pesto

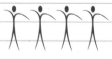

Servings

10 oz. (300 g) corn tagliatelle – 1 bunch of basil – 1 garlic clove – 2 1/2 tbsp (20 g) pine nuts – 20 pine nuts for decorating the pasta – 1/4 cup (30 g) grated Pecorino cheese – 3 tbsp (about 30 g) extra virgin olive oil – salt and pepper

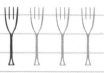

Difficulty

1. Trim the basil, wash the leaves and dry them by dabbing with paper towels or a dishcloth. Peel the garlic and mince.

2. Crush the pine nuts in a mortar and transfer into a bowl. Place the basil leaves in the mortar as well, crush the leaves gently obtaining an aromatic paste. Add them to the pine nuts. Add the cheese, garlic, salt and pepper to taste, and mix.

Prep Time
10 minutes

3. If you have a lot of basil, you can prepare a large amount of pesto and store it in hermetic storage jars or the freezer.

4. Cook the corn pasta following the cooking times indicated on the packaging. Drain and add to the pesto. Finally, add whole pine nuts and serve.

Cooking Time
5-10 minutes

This dish is perfect in the summer and is also excellent at room temperature.

Whole Wheat Pasta with Asparagus

Servings

10 oz. (300 g) whole wheat pasta - 10 oz. (300 g) asparagus tips - 1 shallot - 2 egg yolks - 1/4 cup (50 g) soy cream - 2 tbsp (about 20 g) extra virgin olive oil - salt and pepper

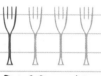

Difficulty

Prep Time
10 minutes

Cooking Time
10 minutes

1. Wash the asparagus and slice. Peel and finely slice the shallot.

2. Pour the oil into a non-stick frying pan. As soon as it heats up, add the shallot and sauté for 2 minutes. Add the asparagus. Cook for about 3-4 minutes while stirring, adding a tablespoon of water if needed, then add the soy cream. Season with salt and pepper, and take off the heat.

3. Cook the pasta of your choice in boiling water following instructions on the packaging.

4. Drain and transfer into the frying pan with the sauce. Set back over heat. Add the egg yolks, mix and serve.

Tomatoes Stuffed with Brown Rice

Servings

4 ripe and firm tomatoes - 1 1/2 cups (300 g) cooked brown rice - 3.5 oz. (100 g) white string beans - 10 walnut kernels - 1 white onion - 4 tbsp (about 40 g) extra virgin olive oil - salt and pepper

Difficulty

Prep Time
15 minutes

Cooking Time
20 minutes

1. Preheat the oven to 390 degrees F (200 degrees C). Wash the tomatoes and gently hollow them out, placing the pulp into a bowl. Pass the pulp through a sieve keeping only the juice. In the meanwhile, drain the tomato shells by setting them upside down on a cutting board. Peel and finely chop the onion. Wash the white string beans and chop into small pieces.

2. Place the rice, beans, coarsely chopped walnuts and onions into a frying pan and toast the ingredients for 5 minutes over high heat, bathing with the tomato juice one tablespoon at a time. Be careful: the filling should not be too moist.

3. Oil a baking sheet as well as the tomatoes arranged on top. Stuff the tomatoes with the seasoned rice and bake for 20 seconds. Serve hot.

Radicchio with Turmeric Rice Tagliolini

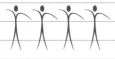

Servings

2 heads of radicchio – 10 oz. (300 g) rice tagliolini – 1 tbsp (about 9 g) powdered turmeric – 3.5 oz. (100 g) zucchini cut into thin sheets – 1/4 cup (20 g) almonds – 4 tbsp (about 60 ml) soy cream – 4 tbsp (about 40 g) extra virgin olive oil – 1 rosemary sprig – 8 sage leaves – edible flowers to taste – salt and pepper

Difficulty

1. Wash the radicchio and remove the larger leaves, which you will use as the base for your dish later. Place all the other leaves into a bowl and season with 2 tablespoons of oil, salt and pepper shortly before cooking the rice tagliolini.

Prep Time
15 minutes

2. Prepare the seasoning for the pasta. Pour the remaining oil, soy cream, coarsely chopped almonds and the zucchini slices into a frying pan. As soon as they heat up, add the turmeric, salt and pepper to taste. Mix and add 4 tablespoons of boiling water. Cook over very low heat for 3-4 minutes.

Cooking Time
10 minutes

3. Prepare four plates, arranging the large radicchio leaves on the bottoms. Cook the pasta in boiling water for the time indicated on the packaging then drain. Add to the frying pan containing the condiment and toss over low heat until the pasta is fully coated with the condiment. Add half of the herbs. Arrange the pasta on top of the radicchio leaves and place some seasoned radicchio on the side. Decorate with flowers and the remaining herbs.

This dish allows you to benefit fully from radicchio's properties, which remain unaltered in the raw leaves.
In addition, the contrast between the hot aroma of the pasta and the refreshing bitterness of the salad is delightful!

Venere Rice with Curry

Servings

3/4 cup (150 g) Venere rice – 1/2 cup (100 g) oat cream –
1 tbsp (about 9 g) curry – 1 purple onion – 1 garlic clove –
1 eggplant – 2 tbsp (about 20 g) extra virgin olive oil – salt

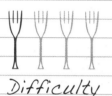

Difficulty

Prep Time
20 minutes

Cooking Time
20 minutes

1. Place the rice into a pot and add double the
volume of water. Cook covered for 10 minutes
(or the time needed for all the water to be
absorbed). This cooking method will ensure the
rice is cooked to the correct degree despite the
short cooking time. Set aside for at least one
hour before using.

2. Trim all the vegetables. Finely chop the onion
and mince the garlic. Dice the eggplant and
sprinkle with a tablespoon of salt.

3. Pour the oil into a wide non-stick frying pan.
Once hot, add the onion and the garlic. Sweat
over low heat for a few minutes then add the
diced eggplant (washed and dried). Cook a little
longer. In the meanwhile, dissolve the curry in
the cream and add to the eggplant. Season with
salt to taste.

4. Add the rice and cook for 2-3 more minutes to
blend the flavors of all the ingredients. Serve.

Whole Wheat Tagliolini
with Crustaceans and Capers

Servings

For the tagliolini: 2 cups (250 g) whole wheat flour – 2 eggs
For the sauce: 2 garlic cloves – 1 fresh chili pepper –
1 purple onion – 2 tbsp (about 20 g) minced herbs (oregano,
basil, thyme and rosemary) – 10 capers in salt – 10 large
shrimp – 10 langoustines – 4 tbsp (about 40 g) extra virgin
olive oil – salt

Difficulty

1. Blend the flour with the eggs and about 1/4
cup (0.5 dl) of water. Knead the ingredients on a
comfortable working surface or in a planetary
mixer. If the amount of water is not sufficient,
add some more one tablespoon at a time. Once the
dough is homogeneous, roll it out into sheets
first and then cut into small, thin strips
following your preference. Let sit on a floured
surface until needed.

Prep Time
50 minutes

2. Mince the capers without rinsing the salt.
Wash the crustaceans and make a cut along the
carapace with scissors so that once cooked,
they are easier to open and enjoy.

3. Prepare the condiment by peeling and mincing the
onion and garlic. Pour the oil into a somewhat
large frying pan and add some flavor with sliced
chili pepper if you prefer more spice. If not,
leave the chili pepper whole.

Cooking Time
10 minutes

4. Add the bulb vegetables and the herbs. Cook for 2
minutes while stirring. Add the crustaceans and
cook for an additional 1-2 minutes. Season with
salt (a very small amount will suffice because of
the salt of the capers!). Take of the heat and cover.

5. Boil the tagliatelle for a few minutes. Drain
so they remain slightly moist and add to the
condiment. Mix and serve.

Legume Cake

1/2 cup (100 g) boiled yellow soy beans – 1/2 cup (100 g) boiled white beans – 2/3 cup (100 g) boiled and drained chickpeas – 1 cup (200 g) boiled Venere rice – 1/2 cup (100 g) oat cream – 1 onion – 2 carrots – 1 red bell pepper – 3 tbsp (about 30 g) extra virgin olive oil – 7 oz. (200 g) premade whole wheat dough – salt and pepper

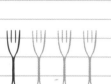

Difficulty

1. Peel and finely slice the onion. Wash and grate the carrots. Wash, trim and finely chop the bell pepper.

2. After preheating to oven to 390 degrees F (200 degrees C), line a baking pan with parchment paper. Roll out the premade dough and use it to coat the baking pan.

Prep Time
15 minutes

3. Place all the ingredients into a bowl, mix, season with oil, oat cream, salt and pepper to taste, and transfer into the baking pan. Fold the excess dough over the filling and bake.

4. Leave in for about 20-30 minutes then take out of the oven. Allow to cool for 5 minutes before removing from the baking pan and cutting.

Cooking Time
30 minutes

Purple Potato Cake with Cereal and Pistachios

Servings

4 purple potatoes – 2 yellow potatoes – 1 onion – 1/4 cup (50 g) pearled barley – 1 zucchini – 1 tbsp (about 10 g) minced parsley – 2 eggs – 1/2 cup (100 g) whole yogurt similar to Greek – 1 tbsp (about 15 g) chopped pistachios – 20 whole pistachios – 4 tbsp (about 40 g) extra virgin olive oil – salt and pepper

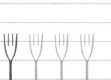

Difficulty

1. Wash the potatoes and slice three of them, one yellow and two purple. If possible, use an electric slicer to get thin, moldable slices. Peel and chop the other potatoes. Boil them. Wash the barley and cook in boiling water for about 30 minutes then drain. Trim the zucchini and grate it. Peel and finely slice the onion.

Prep Time
25 minutes

2. Pour the yogurt into a bowl and blend it with the eggs, chopped potatoes, barley, chopped pistachios, zucchini and onion. Season with salt and pepper to taste.

3. After preheating the oven to 390 degrees F (200 degrees C), pour the oil into a container and dip the potato slices in it. Line the bottom and sides of a baking sheet with a diameter of about 10 in. (25 cm) first with parchment paper then with the potato slices. Pour in the filling and bake for 30 minutes.

Cooking Time
30 minutes

4. Before serving, allow the cake to cool for 5 minutes and decorate with whole pistachios.

Rice Cake with Legumes

Servings

1 cup (200 g) boiled brown rice – 1 cup (200 g) shucked beans – 2 carrots – 1 onion – 1/2 cup (100 g) soy cream – 2 tbsp (about 20 g) minced herbs (rosemary, thyme and oregano) – 1 tbsp (about 20 g) tomato paste – 2 tbsp (about 20 g) extra virgin olive oil – 1/2 cup (50 g) breadcrumbs – salt and pepper

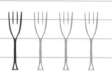

Difficulty

1. Wash and dice the carrots. Peel and slice the onion. Wash and drain the beans. Dissolve the tomato paste in 3/4 cup (2 dl) of water.

2. Place the oil, onion and carrots into a frying pan. Mix and gently sauté. Next, add the beans and cover. Bathe every so often with the tomato water. Leave over heat for about 40 minutes then reduce the liquid and take off the heat.

Prep Time
10 minutes

3. Mix together the herbs and the breadcrumbs in a bowl then preheat the oven to 390 degrees F (200 degrees C). Grease a baking pan of a shape of your choice and coat the sides and bottom with the breadcrumbs.

4. Pour the rice into a bowl, add the soy cream, salt, pepper and the remaining herbs.

Cooking Time
70 minutes

5. Add to the cooked vegetables in the frying pan then transfer into the baking pan. Bake for about 30 minutes. Allow to cool before serving directly in the baking pan or on a serving plate.

Creamy Asparagus Soup with Croutons and Crunchy Vegetables

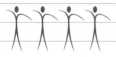

Servings

4 1/4 cups (1 l) vegetable broth – 14 oz. (400 g) asparagus –
1 potato – 1 onion – 4 tbsp (about 40 g) extra virgin olive oil –
salt and pepper – 8 slices of toasted whole wheat bread
For the crunchy vegetables: 1 carrot – 1 chili pepper –
10 arugula leaves – 1 asparagus

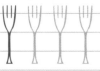

Difficulty

**Prep Time
10 minutes**

**Cooking Time
30 minutes**

1. To prepare the crunchy vegetables, wash and dry the vegetables. Peel the carrot and asparagus with a vegetable peeler. Slice the chili pepper into matchsticks and remove all but the central stem from the arugula. Arrange the vegetables on a baking sheet and dry in the oven at 300 degree F (150 degree C) for 10 minutes. Turn over and check to make sure they are dry. If not, leave in the oven for longer.

2. Trim the asparagus. Remove the tough, woody bottom and break into pieces. Peel and dice the potato. Peel and slice the onion.

3. Pour the oil into a frying pan. Add the vegetables and the broth. Boil until the vegetables are soft and break apart when mashed with a fork (about 30 minutes). Season with salt and pepper once cooked.

4. Blend the mixture. If it is too liquid, place back over heat for an additional ten minutes. Right before serving, divide the creamy soup between diners, accompany with the toasted bread and crunchy vegetables, and serve hot.

Onion and Chickpea Soup

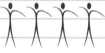

Servings

4 white onions or shallots – 1 cup (200 g) dried chickpeas –
1 tbsp (about 10 g) minced rosemary – 4 slices of stale
whole wheat bread – 1/2 cup (50 g) grated Parmigiano cheese –
salt and pepper

Difficulty

1. Wash and drain the chickpeas after soaking
them for at least 8-10 hours. Peel and slice
the onions.

2. Boil the chickpeas and the onions in 6 cups (1.5 l)
of water, adding half of the minced rosemary.
Cover and cook for at least 2 hours or until the
chickpeas are soft. Season with salt and pepper
to taste. Once the soup is ready, when the liquid
has reduced by about half, take the pot off
the heat.

**Prep Time
20 minutes**

3. Preheat the oven to 390 degrees F (200 degrees C),
take a baking pan and pour in the soup.
Add the bread, sprinkle with Parmigiano,
remaining rosemary and more pepper if desired.
Bake until the cheese has melted (about 5
minutes) and the kitchen is filled with a
delicious and irresistible aroma!

**Resting Time
10 hours**

4. Take out of the oven and serve immediately,
while still hot.

**Cooking Time
65 minutes**

Mains...

Protein should make up at least 15-25% of our daily calorie intake. Thanks to the amino acids they contain, proteins are essential for the development and maintenance of muscles, as well as for cognitive functions. It is best to use proteins derived from free-range animals, rather than industrial, replacing whole milk with skimmed, and using organic eggs. Due to the lower fat content, white meat and fish are preferable to red meat. Fish is white meat and is ideal because in addition to providing protein, it is rich in the valuable omega-3, essential fatty acids for combatting cognitive decline, as well as improving mood and ability to concentrate. Oily fish is less exposed to sources of pollution and therefore contains less contaminants. For those who follow a vegetarian or vegan diet, legumes - especially beans and soybeans - are the best source of plant-based protein in the world!

Asparagus, Egg and Ricotta Bake

Servings

10 oz. (300 g) asparagus tips – 2 eggs – 3/4 cup (200 g) goat's milk ricotta – 7 oz. (200 g) cleaned and seasoned lettuce – salt and pepper

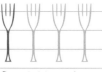

Difficulty

1. Wash the asparagus, steam for 5 minutes and cut into small slices.

2. After preheating the oven to 350 degrees F (180 degrees C), place the ricotta, eggs and sliced asparagus into a bowl. Mix and season with salt and pepper to taste.

3. Line a round baking pan with a diameter of about 8 in. (20 cm) with parchment paper. Pour the mixture into the baking pan and bake for 20 minutes. Allow to cool before serving.

Prep Time
10 minutes

Cooking Time
25 minutes

An excellent dish, perfect for springtime. It is delicious accompanied with a simple lettuce salad.

Bell Pepper Bites with Lettuce Salad

Servings

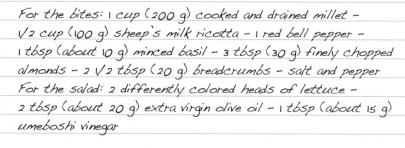

For the bites: 1 cup (200 g) cooked and drained millet –
1/2 cup (100 g) sheep's milk ricotta – 1 red bell pepper –
1 tbsp (about 10 g) minced basil – 3 tbsp (30 g) finely chopped
almonds – 2 1/2 tbsp (20 g) breadcrumbs – salt and pepper
For the salad: 2 differently colored heads of lettuce –
2 tbsp (about 20 g) extra virgin olive oil – 1 tbsp (about 15 g)
umeboshi vinegar

Difficulty

1. Wash the bell pepper. Eliminate the white parts
and the seeds. Finely chop.
Combine the bell pepper, millet, ricotta and
basil in a bowl. Season with salt and pepper
to taste.

2. Pour the breadcrumbs and chopped almonds onto
a flat surface.

**Prep Time
30 minutes**

3. After mixing all the ingredients, use your hands
to shape balls. Coat them with the breading,
making sure it adheres well. Arrange the balls
on a serving plate.

4. Wash and drain the lettuce. Rip into pieces and
place into a salad bowl. Season with oil and
umeboshi vinegar (which is sapid hence, taste
before adding salt).

5. Serve the salad with the bites.

Tomato Cream with Bean Salad

Servings

4 ripe but firm tomatoes – 1 cup (200 g) shucked fresh beans – 1 spring onion – 3.5 oz. (100 g) tofu – 4 fresh basil sprigs – 1 tsp (about 3 g) minced cilantro and cardamom – 1 lemon – 4 tbsp (about 40 g) extra virgin olive oil – salt and pepper

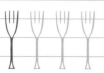

Difficulty

1. Wash the beans and cook them over low heat until they are soft (about one hour should be enough for the right consistency), then drain.

2. Pour the legumes into a bowl. Add 2 tablespoons of oil, and salt and pepper to taste. Cover and set aside until needed. Dice the tofu.

Prep Time
20 minutes

3. Wash the tomatoes, remove the skin and seeds, and place the pulp into a blender. Blend with the remaining olive oil, half of the sliced spring onion, freshly squeezed lemon juice, salt and pepper to taste.

4. Once the cream is soft and homogeneous, transfer onto plates. Spoon the beans flavored with minced cilantro and cardamom, remaining spring onion and basil on top of the cream and serve. If desired, you can drizzle with oil.

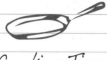

Cooking Time
60 minutes

Whole Wheat Croutons with a Mediterranean Patè

Servings

14 oz. (400 g) whole wheat bread – 1.7 oz. (50 g) sun-dried tomatoes – 1/2 cup (50 g) capers in salt – 1/3 cup (50 g) almonds – 2/3 cup (100 g) extra virgin olive oil – 2 garlic cloves – 1 fresh chili pepper (optional)

Difficulty

1. Soak the tomatoes and the capers separately for 30 minutes in warm water. The latter should be rinsed several times under running water to eliminate excess salt.

2. Gently crush the almonds in a mortar. Peel the garlic.

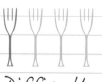

Prep Time
10 minutes

3. Squeeze out the tomatoes, chop and place into a blender along with the capers, garlic, chili pepper (if desired) and oil. Blend for 1 minute (the time may vary with the type of blender!) then add the almonds and blend for a few additional seconds.

4. Transfer into a container and set aside to rest until use.

Cooking Time
10 minutes

5. Slice the bread as thinly as possible and toast in an oven at 390 degrees F (200 degrees C) for 3-4 minutes per side. Serve the croutons with the patè.

Roasted Guinea Fowl with Shallots, Onions and White Wine

Servings

1 Guinea fowl of about 2.5 lb (1200 g) – 1 2/3 cup (4 dl) white wine – 4 garlic cloves – 4 shallots – 4 purple onions – 2 tbsp (about 20 g) extra virgin olive oil

Difficulty

Prep Time
10 minutes

Cooking Time
70 minutes

1. Preheat the oven to 390 degrees F (200 degrees C). Pass the Guinea fowl over open flame to singe any remaining feathers. Wash it, dry and cut into pieces. Wash the shallots and leave the skin on.

2. Pour the oil into a baking pan and add peeled garlic. Heat up on the pan then add the peeled onions, Guinea fowl pieces and the shallots with skin. Brown over high heat for 5 minutes.

3. Bathe with wine, season with salt and pepper to taste and place in the oven. Make sure the meat is cooks evenly by turning the pieces over several times. Bake for about 60-70 minutes then serve.

Sardine Fillets with Caper and Tomato Cream

Servings

1 lb. (500 g) sardines – 1 ripe but firm tomato – 1/4 cup (20 g) almonds – 1 1/2 tbsp (10 g) capers in salt – 0.35 oz. (10 g) wild fennel – 10 pitted olives – 1 garlic clove – 1/4 cup (0.5 dl) extra virgin olive oil – 1 minced dried chili pepper – salt

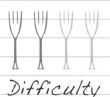

Difficulty

1. Trim and chop the wild fennel. Place it into a bowl. Remove excess salt from the capers without washing them. Mince and add to the wild fennel. Peel the garlic and mince with the olives. Add to the other ingredients.

2. Coarsely chop the almonds as well and add to the rest. Mix and season with salt (remembering that the capers are already very salty!). Flavor with chili pepper and season with oil.

**Prep Time
20 minutes**

3. Peel the tomato, remove the seeds and chop. Set aside to drain in a colander. Wash the sardines. Remove the insides and the spine then divide into fillets. Dry with paper towels.

4. Heat a non-stick frying pan and brown the sardines for 2 minutes per side. Transfer onto a serving dish one at a time as soon as they are done. Finally, spoon the condiment and chopped tomatoes on top.

**Cooking Time
5 minutes**

Mackerel Fillets with Capers

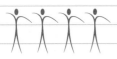

Servings

4 mackerel fillets – 10 capers in oil – 4 steamed purple potatoes – 4 tomatoes – 2 garlic cloves – 2 tbsp (about 20 g) extra virgin olive oil – salt and pepper

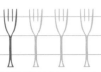

Difficulty

Prep Time
10 minutes

Cooking Time
25 minutes

1. Preheat the oven to 390 degrees F (200 degrees C) and oil a baking pan large enough to fit the fish.

2. Slice the potatoes. Wash the tomatoes and cut them into 1/16 in. (2 mm) thick slices. Peel and mince the garlic.

3. Pour a thin layer of oil into the baking pan. Arrange a layer of potatoes and tomatoes and top with the mackerel.

4. Flavor with capers and minced garlic. Cover with the remaining vegetables. Season with salt and pepper, add the remaining oil and bake for 25 minutes.

5. Once cooked, take out of the oven and divide between diners.

Bell Peppers and Eggplants Stuffed with Sardines

Servings

1 bell pepper – 1 eggplant – 10 oz. (300 g) sardines – 1 cup (200 g) quinoa – 2 tbsp (about 20 g) minced herbs (parsley, oregano, marjoram and mint) – 4 tbsp (about 40 g) extra virgin olive oil – 2 tbsp (about 22 ml) apple vinegar

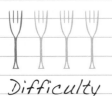

Difficulty

1. Cook the quinoa covered in double its volume of water. After 10 minutes, take off the heat and set aside for at least 30 minutes with the cover on.

2. Pour 2 cups (0.5 l) of water and vinegar into a low and wide pan. Insert the steaming insert. Wash the bell pepper and cut into strips, removing the white sections and the seeds. Wash and slice the eggplant. Drizzle with salt to draw out the water. After 5 minutes, wash once more and dry.

Prep Time
20 minutes

3. Cook the vegetables over low heat for about 20 minutes then set aside to air-dry.

4. Gut and wash the sardines. Steam them separately. After about 20 minutes, take them out of the steamer and remove the spine. Add them to the quinoa and season with oil, herbs, salt and pepper to taste.

Resting Time
30 minutes

Cooking Time
20 minutes

5. Use the resulting mixture to fill the eggplant slices and bell pepper strips. Place the stuffed vegetables on a serving plate and serve at room temperature.

Purple Potato Croquettes

Servings

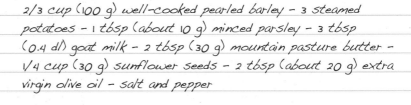

2/3 cup (100 g) well-cooked pearled barley - 3 steamed potatoes - 1 tbsp (about 10 g) minced parsley - 3 tbsp (0.4 dl) goat milk - 2 tbsp (30 g) mountain pasture butter - 1/4 cup (30 g) sunflower seeds - 2 tbsp (about 20 g) extra virgin olive oil - salt and pepper

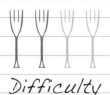

Difficulty

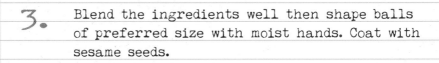

1. Preheat the oven to 390 degrees F (200 degrees C). Grease a baking sheet with olive oil.

2. Mash the potatoes and mix them with the barley in a bowl. Add the parsley, butter and goat milk. Season with salt and pepper to taste.

3. Blend the ingredients well then shape balls of preferred size with moist hands. Coat with sesame seeds.

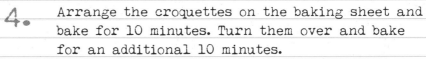

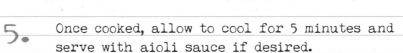

**Prep Time
20 minutes**

4. Arrange the croquettes on the baking sheet and bake for 10 minutes. Turn them over and bake for an additional 10 minutes.

5. Once cooked, allow to cool for 5 minutes and serve with aioli sauce if desired.

**Cooking Time
20 minutes**

Vegetable Platter with Aioli Dip

Servings

4 garlic cloves - 2 tbsp (about 30 ml) lemon juice -
1 cup (250 g) sunflower oil - 2 egg yolks - salt and pepper -
vegetables in season (carrots, spring onions, broccoli, bell
peppers etc.)

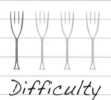

Difficulty

1. Peel the garlic cloves and crush them in a
   mortar. Pour the egg yolks into a bowl.
   Add the garlic and a pinch of salt and pepper.
   Beat using an immersion blender with a whisk
   attachment while drizzling in the oil.

2. Once you have a shiny, compact cream, dilute
   with the lemon juice. Season with salt and
   pepper, and store in the fridge until needed.

3. Trim, wash, dry and chop the vegetables.

**Prep Time
20 minutes**

4. Spoon the dip into a serving dish and accompany
   with the vegetables and, if desired, toasted
   bread.

Trout Pastries

Servings

1 lb. (500 g) wild trout fillet – 2 heads of radicchio – 2 carrots – 1 lemon – 10 capers in oil – 4 tbsp (about 40 g) extra virgin olive oil – chili pepper – salt

Difficulty

Prep Time
20 minutes

Marinating Time
10 minutes

1. Remove any remaining bones or skin from the trout fillets. Use a very sharp knife to cut the fillets into the thinnest slices possible and place them onto a plate.

2. Drizzle the trout slices with freshly squeezed lemon juice. Season with salt and add a few pieces of chili pepper. Set aside to marinate for about 10 minutes then drain.

3. Wash the radicchio and the carrots. Cut the carrots into small strips and finely chop the radicchio. Using a plating ring, layer the various ingredients (carrots, radicchio and fish) and top with 2-3 unwashed capers and a tablespoon of oil for more flavor.

4. Remove the ring right before serving.

Broccoli and Radicchio Bake

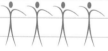

Servings

7 oz. (200 g) broccoli - 1 head of radicchio - 4 eggs - 3/4 cup (200 g) non dairy cream - 4 tbsp (about 40 g) extra virgin olive oil - 2 garlic cloves - salt and pepper

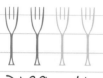

Difficulty

1. Preheat the oven to 320 degrees F (160 degrees C). Trim, wash and dry the vegetables. Chop the broccoli into small pieces and slice the radicchio.

2. Pour the oil into a somewhat large frying pan. Add aroma with freshly crushed garlic and after one minute add the vegetables. Cook over medium heat with the cover on for about 10 minutes. Take out the garlic and coarsely chop the vegetables.

Prep Time
15 minutes

3. Place the vegetables into a bowl. Add the cream and the eggs. Season with salt and pepper to taste. Mix until the ingredients are well blended. Grease single portion baking molds and pour in the mixture 2/3 of the way up.

Cooking Time
30 minutes

4. Bake for about 30 minutes (until the contents have risen to the edge of the containers). Turn off the oven and allow to cool. Before serving, heat up the molds in a water bath for 2-3 minutes then flip them onto a plate.

Vacuum-cooked Turkey with Spices and Herbs

Servings

14 oz. (400 g) turkey – 3 tbsp (about 30 g) minced herbs (fresh thyme, oregano, rosemary and marjoram) – 1 onion – 2 carrot – 1 chili pepper – 4 cloves – 1 garlic clove – 10 pepper kernels – 4 tbsp (about 40 g) extra virgin olive oil

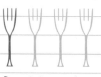

Difficulty

1. Take out a 16 oz. (0.5 l) container. Bring 8 1/2 cups (2 l) of water to a boil in a pot.

2. Remove any fatty sections from the meat and set it on a cutting board. In the center, place the cloves, pepper kernels, half of the chili pepper, half of the coarsely chopped onion, a tablespoon of herbs and a carrot.

Prep Time
10 minutes

3. Roll up the meat, coat with the remaining herbs and place into the container. Add the remaining ingredients. Close and set into the pot. Bring to a boil and cook for 10 minutes. Once the heat is off, wait for the water to cool.

4. Right before serving, take the dish out of the pot and slice the turkey meat. Season with oil and lemon juice if desired.

Resting Time
30 minutes

Cooking Time
10 minutes

Juices and Smoothies...

A balanced diet doesn't have to be limited to meals at home. Thanks to juices and smoothies, you can also take advantage of the nutritional quality of "smart" foods in the middle of a working day, or when you have little time to cook elaborate dishes. However, it is important to choose the ingredients carefully depending on your recommended calorie intake and your needs. For example, cocoa and goat's milk or green tea, banana and persimmon are great for athletes. Goat's milk reintegrates the proteins necessary for the muscles to recover after vigorous exercise, while the potassium content in bananas is ideal to prevent muscle cramps. Use soy milk if you want lots of proteins and few fats. Smoothies that combine fruit and vegetables are incredible vitamin cocktails, rich in antioxidants. Thanks to the fibre in fruit and vegetables, smoothies make an excellent low-calorie snack that makes you feel pleasantly full.

Strawberry and Lettuce Smoothie

Servings

3 cups (400 g) ripe strawberries – 1 head of lettuce – 1 lemon

Difficulty

**Prep Time
10 minutes**

1. Trim the strawberries eliminating the stem and chop directly into the blender jar into as many pieces as the berry size requires.

2. Trim, wash and tear up the lettuce while still moist. Juice in a juice extractor.

3. Catch the juice, mix it with freshly squeezed lemon juice and add to the rest.

4. Turn on the blender and once the mixture is fluid and velvety, pour into glasses.

An excellent thirst quencher and energy booster, it is also great with a few ice cubes. You can also use frozen strawberries for a sorbet-like texture.

Cucumber, Bell Pepper and Tomato Smoothie

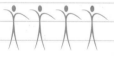

Servings

Difficulty

**Prep Time
5 minutes**

2 cucumbers – 2 ripe tomatoes – 1 red bell pepper –
2 tbsp (about 20 g) extra virgin olive oil – 4 garlic sprouts –
salt and pepper – 10 basil leaves

1. Trim the vegetables. Peel the tomatoes and half of the cucumbers. If you want a lighter colored smoothie, remove the skin from all the cucumbers. Remove the seeds and white sections from the bell pepper.

2. Chop the ingredients.

3. Place all the ingredients (except the garlic sprouts), the oil, basil, and salt and pepper to taste into the blender jar. Blend with 10 ice cubes.

4. Divide between the diners and place a fresh garlic sprout into each glass to flavor and add aroma to the mixture. The smell and flavor of the sprouts are less intense than those of ripe garlic, however their inviting aroma whets the appetite.

This smoothie is deliciously refreshing, recommended during hot summer months, and perfect at any time of the day, especially as a first course substitute. Its elevated fiber contents help during weight loss diets, leaving a pleasant feeling of fullness in spite of a truly low amount of calories!

Persimmon Chocolate Smoothie with Goat Milk

Servings

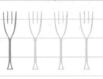

Difficulty

**Prep Time
5 minutes**

4 persimmons – 1 tbsp (about 15 g) cocoa powder – 1 2/3 cups (4 dl) goat milk – 1 tbsp (about 10 g) honey

1. Dissolve the cocoa powder and the honey in warm milk.

2. Wash the persimmons, remove the skin, seeds and stem. Blend then add the milk and continue blending until creamy and velvety.

3. Transfer into glasses and serve.

This smoothie gives a boost of energy making it a perfect nutritious breakfast for students, athletes and everyone who needs to stay concentrated and keep up their energy levels for long periods. It is also an excellent way to get your strength back after a strenuous workout.

Apple, Avocado and Chili Pepper Smoothie

Servings

4 apples – 1 fresh chili pepper – 1/2 cup (1 dl) soy milk – 3.5 oz. (100 g) avocado – 1 lemon

Difficulty

1. Wash the apples. Chop and place into a blender. Add freshly squeezed lemon juice.

2. After washing the chili pepper (chosen based on desired spiciness), remove the filaments and the seeds (which are often very spicy) and add to the other ingredients.

3. Cut the avocado directly into the blender, dilute with milk and blend until fluid and homogeneous.

**Prep Time
10 minutes**

For a more decisive flavor, add a pinch of salt and a tablespoon of extra virgin olive oil. An excellent substitute for a high-energy, tasty and thirst-quenching snack. The ingredients of this smoothie grant a feeling of fullness and are recommended for weight loss diets.

Apple Smoothie with Carrots, Cabbage and Orange

Servings

1 orange – 2 apples – 3.5 oz. (100 g) red cabbage – 2 carrots – 1 lemon – 1 tsp (about 3 g) extra virgin olive oil – 10 fresh oregano leaves – salt and pepper

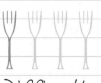

Difficulty

**Prep Time
10 minutes**

1. Wash all the fruits and vegetables. Juice the lemon and pour the juice into the blender. Chop the apples and add them to the juice. Juice the orange and add to the other ingredients.

2. Chop the carrots and the cabbage into small pieces. Add to the rest. Season with oil, oregano, salt and pepper.

3. Add half a glass of water to the mixture and blend.

4. Once the mixture is homogeneous (depending on the blender, you may need from 30 seconds to one minute), pour into glasses and serve.

Oil is recommended for facilitating the absorption of fat-soluble vitamins such as A. As an alternative, you can substitute the oil with nuts.

Spinach Smoothie with Walnuts and Soy Milk

Servings

2 1/3 cups (100 g) spinach – 10 walnuts – 1 2/3 cups (4 dl) soy milk

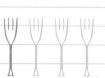

Difficulty

Prep Time
10 minutes

1. Trim, wash and gently drain the spinach.

2. Crack the walnuts and place the kernels into the blender along with the spinach and the soy milk.

3. Blend for a few seconds, just the time necessary for a homogeneous mixture, then pour into glasses and serve.

This smoothie is flavorful and rich in nutrients. It can be stored for a few hours in cool location in an airtight container. It is excellent as a light first course or a tasty and original appetizer.

Wild Berry Smoothie

Servings

3 1/2 cups (500 g) berries (raspberries, blueberries, blackberries and currants) – 1/2 cup (1 dl) apple juice – 1 banana

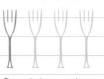

Difficulty

1. Trim all the berries and freeze while still moist.

2. After 2 hours in the freezer, transfer into the blender.

3. Add the apple juice and sliced banana and blend.

4. Once the mixture is creamy and soft, transfer into cups or glasses and serve.

**Prep Time
5 minutes**

Smoothies prepared with frozen fruit have a magnificent texture. This smoothie is recommended above all for those who do not enjoy eating fruit and is a perfect snack for kids or as a thirst-quencher on a hot summer day.

Almond Milk with Kiwi and Chokeberries

Servings

1 1/4 cups (3 dl) almond milk – 4 kiwis – 3 tbsp (30 g) chokeberries

Difficulty

1. Soften the chokeberries in lukewarm almond milk.

2. Wash, peel and chop the kiwis.

3. Place into a blender. Add the almond milk with the chokeberries and blend until all the ingredients are well blended.

**Prep Time
10 minutes**

4. Pour into glasses and serve.

Thirst-quenching, energetic and rich in vitamins and minerals, this is a very pleasant beverage suitable for rehydrating after a workout or for active and vivacious children.

Red Orange Juice with Fennel

Servings

4 blood oranges - 1 organic apple - 2 fennels - salt and pepper

Difficulty

1. Trim, wash and chop the fennels.

2. Peel the oranges. Juice two and cut the others into slices removing the white membranes.

3. Wash and chop the apples. Do not peel.

4. Blend until creamy and homogeneous.

Prep Time
10 minutes

You can season the beverage with salt and pepper to serve as an appetizer or a quick meal, or leave it as is. In either case, it is thirst-quenching, pleasant and refreshing. Thanks to its fiber contents, it leaves a pleasant feeling of fullness.

Radicchio and Lemon Juice

Servings

7 oz. (200 g) radicchio - 2 pears - 1 moderately spicy chili pepper - 1 tsp (about 3g) extra virgin olive oil - 1 lemon - salt

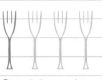

Difficulty

1. Wash, peel and chop the pears. Place into a blender.

2. Add trimmed and washed radicchio, chili pepper (after having removed the stem and seeds), and the oil. Drizzle in freshly squeezed lemon juice.

3. Leave the blender on until the mixture is soft and fluid. If desired, you can dilute the mixture with a glass of cool water.

Prep Time
5 minutes

The sweetness of the pears attenuates the bitterness of the radicchio, while the chili pepper accents the other flavors. The sweet, spicy, bitter and sour flavor combination can be completed with a pinch of salt. The juice retains all the fiber and components of the ingredients. Excellent for rehydrating, substituting a meal or as a healthy aperitif.

Grape Juice with Plum Puree

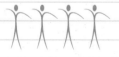

Servings

2 cups (300 g) black grape berries – 14 oz. (400 g) plums – 2 tbsp (20 g) chokeberries – 5 almonds

Difficulty

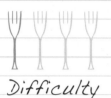

Prep Time
10 minutes

1. Soak the chokeberries in a glass of warm water.

2. Juice the grape berries in a juice extractor (if you don't have one, puree the berries in a blender and pass through a fine mesh strainer).

3. Wash the plums and eliminate the pits. Chop and place into a blender. Blend with the grape juice, chokeberries in their soaking water, and the almonds.

4. Blend until the mixture is fluid and homogeneous then pour into glasses.

If you would like a more thirst-quenching beverage in addition to a source of vitamins and minerals, add 5-6 ice cubes. The almonds, which are tasty in themselves, facilitate the assimilation of fat-soluble vitamins thanks to their oil contents.

Green Tea with Banana and Persimmon

Servings

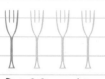

Difficulty

Prep Time
10 minutes

Resting Time
5 minutes

Cooking Time
5 minutes

1 tsp (3 g) green tea – 1 banana – 1 persimmon – 1 small piece of ginger

1. Bring 1 cup (0.25 l) of water to a boil. Pour in the tea and filter after 5 minutes.

2. Cover and set aside to cool.

3. Grate the ginger and gather about one teaspoonful. Peel the banana. Slice and place into the blender. Add the ginger.

4. Wash and peel the persimmon. Remove any seeds and the stem. Add to the blender. Pour in the tea and blend until the beverage is creamy and homogeneous.

5. Serve in glasses.

In addition to providing a boost of energy, this beverage can be an excellent thirst-quencher, just add 5-6 ice cubes to the mixture.

Cherry Yogurt Smoothie

Servings

3 1/3 cups (500 g) cherries - 3/4 cup (200 g) whole yogurt

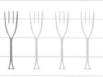

Difficulty

1. Wash the cherries and remove the pits, dropping the berries directly into the blender to ensure none of the juice is lost.

2. Add the yogurt and blend.

3. Once you have a soft cream, pour into glasses and serve.

Prep Time
5 minutes

For a simple and tasty dessert, place the pitted cherries into the freezer and puree while still frozen: the result is a creamy and mouthwatering sorbet! If on the other hand you would like to rehydrate after a workout, add a glass of water per person. The beverage will become a truly tasty thirst-quencher.

The Author

A naturopath, freelance journalist and photographer specializing in wine and food itineraries, CINZIA TRENCHI has collaborated in the writing of numerous recipe books published by Italian and foreign publishing houses. A passionate cook, she has also worked for many Italian magazines covering regional, traditional, macrobiotic and natural cuisine specialties, providing both the text and the photographs, and including dishes of her own creation. Her recipe books include original and creative meals. They propose new flavor associations and unusual pairings that result in unique preparations that keep with the spirit of flavor without forgetting the nutritional properties of foods, in order to achieve the best equilibrium during a meal and the consequent improvement in well-being. She lives in Monferrato, in the Piedmont region, in a home immersed in greenery. Using the flowers, aromatic herbs and vegetables grown in her garden, she prepares original sauces and condiments, in addition to decorations for her dishes, allowing herself to be guided by the seasons and her knowledge of the earth's fruits. In the past years, she has realized several books for White Star Publishers, with great enthusiasm and creativity.

Index of Ingredients

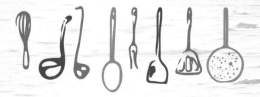

WHITE STAR PUBLISHERS

WS White Star Publishers® is a registered trademark
property of White Star s.r.l.

© 2017 White Star s.r.l.
Piazzale Luigi Cadorna, 6 - 20123 Milan, Italy
www.whitestar.it

Translation and Editing: TperTradurre s.r.l.

ISBN 978-88-544-1092-3
1 2 3 4 5 6   21 20 19 18 17

Printed in China